Bethany W. Pope

The Horned God

The Horned God
published in the United Kingdom in 2025
by Mica Press & Campanula Books

https://micapress.uk | contact@micapress.uk

ISBN 978-1-869848-43-9
Copyright © Bethany W. Pope 2025

The right of Bethany W. Pope to be identified as the author of this work has been asserted by her in accordance with the Copyright, Designs and Patents Act of 1988.

All rights reserved.

For Xeno

Contents

3) Age + Distance

4) Anthills

5) Speaking In Tongues

7) A Bill Comes Due

9)) A Martian Named Smith

11) A Comedy

12) Olathe, Kansas

14) A Giant Fucking Acorn

16) Muckraker

17) The Horned God

18) Penance

19) Cornucopia

20) The Sights

21) Eight Mile Gap

22) Pastoral

23) Egg

Age + Distance

You want to make something — lucid,
and startlingly bright, glimmering
like the blood-sheened proboscis
of a Jurassic mosquito, suspended
in a blob of polished amber — as though
the ancient wounding barb your flesh
cannot seem to disgorge could be redeemed
by the words you case it in. Nothing lingers,
in this or any other world, but maybe this
can last a little longer than the heart
it fed upon. Are you still the child,
will you always be the child, with a bruised
right cheek and dirty feet,
crouched in the back of a closet,
amidst the dust of ancient designer dresses
and shiny-bottomed suits,
imagining how you can force him to see you
as something other than a problem
he defines himself by fixing?
At nine, you fantasized about
slicing your own white belly open
and handing him your viscera to scry
a better present in. You have spent
your adulthood sharpening your knife.
Amber is a tree's dried blood: poetry
is the coagulated spew of an author.
What lasts, beyond death, is ultimately
a matter of percentages.

Anthills

The soil comes from deeper down,
the detritus of hollowed corridors
gathered at the lip of the door.
The rooms and paths inside
are scent marked. This one for farming,
this other for young. The large, central
room is where the queen gives birth,
for twenty year stretches, her cloaca
flexing endlessly in the dark.
It is dark down there, unless
the metropolis is collapsed
between two panes of glass.
It's dark, and hot, and well patrolled.
I have nightmares about anthills,
about being trapped in tunnels,
or cities I don't know. I tend to have
nightmares about the things that I love.
When I was a kid, ten or eleven,
I'd stick my hand into fire ant metropolises,
I'd spread my fingers out and let the soldiers
latch, front and back, to my skin.
The next morning I'd be littered to the elbows
with small, bright green pustules,
which I'd then pop while the teachers
were gathered around me, pressing in,
praying over me, talking about a God
they didn't really know, but maybe I did,
or maybe that's just what I thought.
I'd think about long, pale white queens,
glowing in the numinous dark.
Sometimes a trail of ants
will get caught in a spiral,
following each other, around
and around, until they fall
and lie where they drop.

Speaking In Tongues

An icon of cheap, brittle plastic
(the texture of a necco wafer)
was pressed into the wet sand of the road.
The pink back, sun-faded and piebald,
caught under the toe of my boot,
snagging me like the time (breaking
into an abandoned house) I misstepped and shot
a three inch nail through my sole. It emerged
through the top, gleaming wetly, with malevolence,
and I hid it from my parents for a week.
I hid it until my sister eventually noticed the smell.
If Christ was pinned to the cross
with a red-iron spike, it would have
been driven in above the ankles.
Anywhere else and the flesh would tear
like a licorice whip, unraveling
from the bone in slick, bright ropes.
Anyway, this was a different kind of icon.
When I flipped over the arched token,
paper Guanyin stared up at me, throned,
and garlanded, pointing towards her chest,
and I was back in Sacred Heart,
sneaking into the rear of the sanctuary
in the middle of the service, with my dog
and my guilty protestantism, fingering
the bakelite beads of the rosaries that dangled
in the shop, like vines, and wondering
how the fuck, exactly, they were supposed to work.
The church was in the Spanish style
(pink tiles, flat roof, a plain, peach spire)
and a garden filled with the kind of rancorous,
untamable vegetation that does well in the heat.
There was a fountain filled with chlorinated water,
bluer than the Virgin's veil, with a gray statue
of Mary standing in it with her arms spread.
Surely goodness and mercy will follow me,
all the days of my life, but I never expected mercy
to show up looking like this. I slipped Guanyin

into my pocket, next to a bead,
a stone, between my keys, and my flesh,
yanked back like a dog on a chain
to something I longed for then, and long for still,
but have never been able to reach.

A Bill Comes Due

I think about the smell of you.
Old Spice, old cigarettes, ashes
and musk, and the sweet astringent
of beer metabolized in spent, cold sweat.
I think about your hair, your curly
black hair, and your bright eyes
in that long, hyperthyroid face.
Long, Marfan's fingers. The time
you accidentally speared my palm
with the burning heart of your Camel
because six-year-old me ran
exactly at thigh level. I think
of what you gave me: a book,
a yellow-handled, child-sized hammer,
a scar on my palm. I think about
the way you sloughed it all off,
first the bank, then your wife,
your daughter, your car, your siblings,
all of us myriad nieces and nephews,
your series of smaller, less responsible jobs,
your days and years at rehab,
your anonymous beds, your humor,
your ability to walk, your capacity
for love. Your mind, your quick,
straight-razor smirk, never would leave you.
You were a blade in the form of a man,
a blade without a handle. You cut
absolutely without intention.
You cut, no matter how, or where
a body touched you. You cut
to the weeping, red marrow.
You left a mark.
And I can't stop thinking
about what five days spent decaying
in the hot, hot sun did to your scent,
your eyes, what was left of your body,
before the cops finally gave up
and forced the door down.

And I can't help but wonder,
did the shape of whatever you intended
at last rise up?

A Martian Named Smith

A hard, cold wisdom is required for goodness to accomplish
good. Goodness without wisdom always accomplishes evil.
                                        -Robert Heinlein

The last time we spoke, you were working
for an off-brand convenience store
on the gulf coast. It was a job
you could get after prison. You pulled
fire down to the white ashes, tapped
the butt out on your sister's living room rug,
and said, 'Since I can't drive, I've got a room
set up in the back. They gave me a cot.
Might as well have a chain around my leg.'
I said something about it being an easy commute,
and you smiled, just a little, a narrow fish hook
jag of the upper lip. It was Christmas,
but you didn't eat. You were as skeletal as usual;
black hair going white, and you kept excusing yourself
to the garage. When you came back, you didn't smell
of booze, but there was a burnt chemical smell
so it was probably meth.

Ten years ago, you met a woman on the internet
and drove out to California (in a stolen car,
without a license) to be with her. Forever.
She never wanted anything IRL,
never expected a visit. She was married, I think.
You came back a month later, on a greyhound,
wrapped in a church basement coat,
and you never answered any questions.

I remember that we talked about Heinlein,
about wanting to touch and be touched,
and the way that you quickly squeezed my breast
after Grandma's funeral. I remember pulling back,
hiding in the cloak room among vestments
that had been shed and piled like skins.
You kept repeating, 'My mother is dead,

my mother is dead. My mother is dead.'
You smelled like vomit and vodka and the nutty,
sour stench shared by all lonely men.

You weren't much of an uncle.
As a father, you were so piss poor
that your only daughter probably won't hear
about your news for another week or so.

When I was eight, you gave me a working tool kit
and taught me how to hammer a nail straight.
The tools were bright yellow, half scale,
but they worked. You taught me how
to unkink a bent spike, how to measure twice,
cut once. You gave me your stained copy
of Stranger In A Strange Land,
when I was too young for it.
You tried to teach me multiplication, but gave up
pretty quick. Every time I did something
my father didn't like, he'd say, 'You are going
to wind up exactly like your Uncle Bill.'

There isn't going to be a funeral.
They found your body five days late,
when the neighbors reported a smell.
You couldn't afford the dignity of the grave
and nobody has offered to pay this tab for you.
And all I can think of, now, is how hurt you were,
through your whole echoing life, how hurt
and how lonely, and how long five days can be
in the heat and the sun.

A Comedy

My father, gesturing with a weighted steak knife,
sitting far too close to my brother, is lost in an argument
with me. We are discussing politics — whether it is possible
to be simultaneously ethical and Republican. I argue,
emphatically, that it's not. My father has compassion
for the men he served with, the soldier he counseled,
in the GI jail, after he got drunk on white liquor
and bashed his toddler's brains out on a cinder block wall.
He feels less for women who walk into Walmart
and walk out with five jugs of baby formula
stuffed under their shirts. It's Christmas, and my grandmother
has expanded the table with a large, pine slab.
She's covered the rough grain of the plank with a white
pleather pad, to protect the table cloth. The table cloth
is also white so that, when my father swoops the serrated
blade of his knife (to underscore his anger, at the women
he's heard about on Fox, but never met) and the sharp edge
penetrates my brother's gym-pumped bicep, the blood stands out.
The blood is unmistakable. The knife sticks out
of the wound and throbs, a little, with my brother's heart.
My father laughs and I'm telling myself that it's shock.
It has to be shock. My brother, his face set in a species of calm,
grasps the warm, weighted handle and pulls the blade out.

Olathe, Kansas

I think about the kid every day.
I think about him every time I see
a dark-haired six-year-old shuffling along
with his hands clasped in front
and his eyes on the road.
I dream about him more
than is probably healthy. I think about
his too-big, sun-faded jean jacket.
I think about his dirty brown trousers,
corduroy shiny along the ass.
I think about his brown little ankles,
rising, naked, out of shoes that looked
like they belonged to somebody else.
I think about the way his tears
tracked clean trails on his cheeks
and how he sniffed them up
into his nose as he walked,
occasionally reaching up,
with his bound hands,
to wipe them away.
I only saw him for a few seconds,
before I took off running
(Birkenstocks flapping against the blacktop)
but the image might as well
be cut into the pale flesh of my brain.
Some moments form scar tissue,
especially when they're cutting into,
rubbing their filth into,
a wound that someone else left there,
which hasn't healed up yet,
and now never will.
He had a dog-collar,
a heavy choke chain, around his neck,
just barely visible beneath the ratty jacket.
The collar was linked up to a pair of testicle
handcuffs. They were made to look like gold.
The bit that's meant to swell
the head of a penis was fed

through the loop in the chain,
and the cuffs that are supposed to put
pressure on a pair of balls
were clamped round his wrists
so that if he tried to run,
he'd choke himself silly.
I thought the old man was his grandfather,
walking the highway behind him,
reading a jug book, I thought that until
he showed me his gun. His gun
was stuck through a leather clutch
that dangled off his belt.
And then I took off running.
Cowardice was part of it, yeah,
no getting around it. Cowardice played a part.
But also I didn't have a cellphone with me
and there was a 7/11 less than a mile
out of the scrub. I shoved aside
a fat, toothless girl who laughed
when I gave my descriptions to Dispatch.
'Was he selling his body?' She laughed
and laughed and I dream about that, too,
that joyless fucking cackle,
because I'd heard that laughter when I'd tried
to tell my social worker
what was happening to me at school.
Fuck that toothless girl.
Fuck the pain that hardened her over.
Fuck that old man with his own fucking gun.
Fuck everyone who'd fucked that child,
or wanted to, or thought about it,
or let it slide.
Fuck the whole goddamned country of America,
that scarifying place that set me to running,
that brutal land I'm running from still.
I think about that kid,
every fucking goddamned day,
and I pray to Jesus he's survived it.
But I don't think that he could have,
and anyway, I'll never know.

A Giant Fucking Acorn

My cousins have a lot of children,
the two of them have twenty between them,
so Christmas is a beggaring time.
The solution turned out to be a White Elephant,
one gift for each person, with a ten dollar limit —
a task that was difficult to achieve in 2018,
and likely, now, absolutely impossible.
At any rate, I drew my cousin's name
out of the bucket, and set about thinking.
What could I get someone who was so vastly different
from myself? Who was so ineffably practical
that they thought that ordinary oak trees were
too ostentatious? Someone who is,
besides, fifteen years older than myself?
But then I remembered that her wedding
was beautiful, that she made the centerpieces herself
out of dusky chocolate-coloured roses,
that she once hid a Whoopee Cushion
in the padding of my mother's wheelchair,
and I wondered if I could find a way to shake her up.
You can find the craziest shit in a Dollar General.
I found a wicker acorn the size of a laundry basket.
It was not a basket. It wasn't for anything.
Just a giant fucking acorn made out of straw
that you had to carry with two arms,
and couldn't comfortably set down anywhere.
It was stupid, and amazing, and I almost wanted
to keep it for myself, but I wrapped it up
in white tissue paper, with a giant red bow,
and I gave it to my cousin. When she undid the paper
(folding it neatly and setting it aside with the rest,
to use again next year) her face opened up
with what can only be described as fear and wonder —
the fear you get when you stand up on a numb leg
and the blood starts flowing. It's the pain that comes
with an end to deprivation. Her eyes and mouth
we're giant O's, and after a minute spent in shock
she started laughing. She was laughing and laughing.

She giggled like a chipmunk at a feast, until her cheeks
were wet and red and her breath was all played out.
And all through the rest of that long Christmas
she held that giant fucking acorn in her lap.

Muckraker

In February the water-troughs grew
thick gray rinds, ice that looked like frozen
foam you could break with a blow from the haft
of a mucking-out shovel. The milk-cows,
Guernseys and Jerseys, drank, swirling pale spit
with brown rust-water. Their muzzles trailed strands
of thick, pearly white that looked beautiful
if you could divorce them from their context.
Divorced from the context of the orphanage,
this farm was as beautiful as the cows
who pressed their huge flanks against my body,
forgetting (or unaware) that I was
small and very human. They had the eyes
of post-coital women; wide and so black
you could see your secret thoughts rising up
through those pools. You could scry your own future.
Standing there, hungry, stroking their coarse flanks,
my jaw swollen, fractured beneath livid
skin, I thought that all I saw was just one
more fantasy: a warm bed, piles of books,
a naked, broad-shouldered man I wasn't
afraid of. A man who'd never worked on
a farm, or stuck his thing where it wasn't
wanted. I drew back, sharp, when a young milker
leaned forward to nuzzle me. At this point
tenderness could only bring forth pain. I
slipped in three inches of part-frozen shit.
The sharp scent rose when I fractured the crust.
I braced myself with the blade of the scoop.
After a while, I went back to shoveling.

The Horned God

A seventeen year old boy
with a scrawny, pedophile mustache,
spent every morning welding milk-cows
to mechanical mouths, suction leeching
cream from their teats. I hated that boy,
and the chaw he spat in my face —
warm and brown as the shit I scooped
with the flat-edged barn shovel.
He lived at home, at his own home,
he just worked for the orphanage,
and he drove to the barn
in his daddy's battered brown ford.
Often there was an off-season deer
in the bed of it, sharp hooves jiggling
against metal and paint at every
bump in the road — a bullet hole
puckering in at the thick base
of the neck. In late spring, flies
skittered across the rubbery
glaze of the eye. A dark wound
that would never blink or startle again.
I watched him take a hatchet to a skull,
once, jostling plates of bone loose
from the brain, his grip strong
against the base of the antlers
as though he were tearing roses up
by the roots. Sometimes the sound of it
wakes me up in the night, the wet
squelch of roots torn through thick mud.
When I wake up, the bones in my jaw
ache with the memory of the blade
of the shovel, of what all else his hands did.
I see the near-weightless feet of a fat
horsefly indenting the jelly of an eye.
We are where we've been, we are
what we've been through.
There's nothing else to it.

Penance

Think of it as trimming a nail, just a little too close,
with a hot iron. The horn buds make a smell as they blacken at their roots,
a bit like immolated hair, or fried blood pudding.
Most people apply or inject a numbing agent, before they start,
but the farm I worked for didn't. The calves were
locked up in A-frames, but I held their heads, one at a time.
I didn't want to be there, doing this. I didn't ask to be there,
but I was. No one listens to what you want, when you're twelve.
You're something like a calf yourself. People do things to you,
lead you places, tie you up,
because they think that you need it, and you
spend the rest of your life trying and failing to atone.
I don't sleep much, but when I do I almost always dream
of red rising up through the edges of a cut.
Injured hands pass on their wounds, as though they have no choice,
as though the story could ever end differently,
as though, if you said no, you wouldn't be burnt
and the calves mutilated anyway.

Cornucopia

Once planted, peanuts will grow
in clusters, in clumps, everywhere
the soil is deep enough to set down roots.
Their round leaves spring from the shaft
in even-numbered clusters; yellow flowers,
resembling pea blossoms, like faces
shrouded in pioneer bonnets. They'll grow,
and grow, returning again and again no matter
how many times the farmer yanks them up.
The earth refills with them like a horn
that can be poured from again, and again,
and never emptied. The legumes,
in their faceted brown shells, spring
from the white roots— clusters of meat,
wrapped in pale hair, festooned with green,
like Botticelli's laurels. They cannot be eradicated,
or ever fully consumed.

The Sights

Pushing my child south,
down the crowded pavement of a city street,
bodies jostling everywhere and the twilight air
redolent with salt, lake water, barbecue
smoke, and roast meat, I saw a man
thrusting his way out of the subway.
He was young: built up in a way that spoke
of heavy lifting that favors the shoulders,
neck, arms, back and chest,
but leaves the legs thin, and sorely wanting.
His torso was an arrow
that pointed at his crotch
and, as an arrow, he glistened.
The woman walking next to me
was also young, and slim enough, draped
in a silk sheath that seemed unlikely in this heat—
her black hair held high and pinned above
a powdered, moon-white neck.
Her lips were red, lustrous as a raw
slice of rump steak, glistening also
with that dark, blood-muscle sheen.
I happened to glance at her as she and I
parted for his passing, and the look on her face
was nothing but hungry. Raw hunger
almost looks like a variety of pain
(it is pain) and the flicker of her eyes
across his body resembled the hunger
of a god for the burnt fat of an offering.
Gone, in a second, the appetite suppressed
beneath the usual masks, and we walked on
in all of our various directions
no one satisfied, or one molecule wiser.

Eight Mile Gap

Everything is smaller, in this in-between place,
wedged between a town and a city,
farms caught beneath the high-speed
railway bridge; terraced hills, packed with lychee trees,
duck-runs threaded through them linking
stream to stream, the ducks themselves jogging, gape-
beaked amongst the bracken,
seeking out good things; rice in the valleys,
heavy brown heads bending to the water as though at prayer,
lotuses packed into ponds, so dense you could walk,
like Christ, across the surface of the water,
balanced on the leaves — or skip-float
to paradise wedged inside a blossom
flicked from Guanyin's pearly fingers.
Crops brim against the temple doors,
brush against the brass roll-call of the ancestors,
send tendrils curling over the legs of the guardians
at the gates, deep green leaves with a purplish
undertone, bright against the cinnabar walls.
Cows standing four feet at the shoulders
rub their copper flanks against the railroad towers,
they curl up to sleep in the shade beneath the overpass,
crowding the sidewalk, exhaling milk and hay
and sweet fruit rinds and they look at you,
sloe-eyed, as you thread your way between their tails.
Everything is smaller here, intensified, forced
to a climax as moments elsewhere never seem to manage,
and you are thrumming with the sound, the smell,
the heat of it all, the steam rising from the surface
of the water, rising from the breath of the cattle,
the sunlight, surreal, magnified and dazzling,
and you are tenderly, beautifully caught.

Pastoral

This breed proliferates, variegated
fur, various body-plans, brindled or blond,
curly, smooth, rough, ragged, black, short,
or long, stocky-legged, gangling, ears perked,
snouts like knives or snubbed like guns.
The only constant is the lack of consistency —
the lone legacy of an ancient lineage.
Some are bred for meat, flesh sauteed
in stews labeled, 'other beef', distinguished
by the layers of fat between the muscles.
Others are companions to old men,
groomed to resemble lions or poodles,
swathed in sweaters and small, bright shoes.
These are the still-living ancestors of pug,
pekinese, Tibetan mastiff, or chow-chow,
branches sprouting from the same warped root —
the gray wolf of the steppe still howling,
deep down in the silt. I named my dog
after a poet who liked to get drunk
on white rice wine and wander
through the mountains, cutting verses into bark.
He would have appreciated the joke.
I scooped my dog out of a muddy gutter,
cleaned off the bike grease, the fifty-odd ticks.
The vet brought her through six weeks of fever,
seizures, the whole damned show.
Now she rolls around on my bed,
long tongue lolling from the side of her mouth,
my son's head suspended on her stomach,
his small hands tangled in her gold.

Egg

There's a picture of my son, just two,
dressed up in light tan silk, pinching a brown egg
between two fingers. He's something of an egg
himself, almost nothing but fragile potential.
Eggs are a promise; of a chicken, or a meal.
You can dye a clutch of eggs red, boil them
with a shock of red paper, to distribute
among your relatives. You can colour them
blue or green or yellow, paint them with lines,
particles and waves, and set them in an Easter basket.
You can watch them straining the cloaca of a hen,
a round head, parting lips. You can pluck them, warm,
from the nest and gently blow free the feathers
and shit. My son is an egg. I brood on him.
I carried him home, without stumbling.
In the photograph, my son is cradling
a representation of himself. He is my promise,
and my terror. My egg is tremulous, capacious,
easily broken. He is painting himself, as I watch,
in vivid colours, preparing to break through
the shell of himself. And I'm watching him,
every moment, with my breath held.

www.ingramcontent.com/pod-product-compliance
Lightning Source LLC
Chambersburg PA
CBHW052039070526
44584CB00020B/3161